T0196072

A Handbook for Life

A Practical Guide to Success and Happiness

Richard London

iUniverse, Inc.
New York   Bloomington

iUniverse books may be ordered through booksellers or by contacting:

iUniverse
1663 Liberty Drive
Bloomington, IN 47403
www.iuniverse.com
1-800-Authors (1-800-288-4677)

Because of the dynamic nature of the Internet, any Web addresses or
links contained in this book may have changed since publication and
may no longer be valid. The views expressed in this work are solely those
of the author and do not necessarily reflect the views of the publisher,
and the publisher hereby disclaims any responsibility for them.

ISBN: 978-1-4401-9263-0 (sc)
ISBN: 978-1-4401-9264-7 (hc)
ISBN: 978-1-4401-9265-4 (ebook)

Printed in the United States of America

iUniverse rev. date: 08/09/2010

Contents

Acknowledgements

This book would not have been possible without the support and encouragement of others. I would like to acknowledge my wife Marianne, friends Vince Williams, Dr. Jerry Fishman, Maureen Ryan Griffin, and Chuck Robbins. A special thank you to Mike Salmen who taught me the true meaning of generosity. I'm also grateful for all of the life experiences, good and bad, that made me who I am today.

Preface

There are many great self help books and courses available today to guide you to wealth, happiness, and success. Many of them will work very well for you if you follow their advice. The problem is that typically they require more of an investment in your time and energy than most people are either willing to or able to provide. As a result, people read them and never apply them in their lives.

This book is different. *A Handbook for Life* maximizes your time and targets key areas to aid you in setting and achieving your goals. Its simple chapter exercises will begin to produce results for you the first day you apply them. Begin using this book today to stop reacting to life's situations and to start living the happier, more fulfilling life you desire.

How Do I Get The Most Out Of This Book?

At the end of each chapter are two exercises. The first exercise can usually be done in five to fifteen minutes; the second is a follow-up that allows you to concentrate on a behavior or mindset for a day or more. To get the most out of this book, take the time to do the exercises and actually think about how they apply to your life. To make it easier for you, full size 8 ½ x 11 pages are available for free at www.AHandbookForLife.com.

You may find that the answers to the exercises in certain chapters seem to overlap. That's OK. Pay attention to recurring themes in your answers. That can help you identify and resolve the most important issues in the least amount of time.

I know that your life is so busy that you may not want to take the time to do the exercises, so here's a compromise for you: If you wish, read through each chapter without completing the exercises. You can probably finish the book in one sitting if you do that.

Then, after reading the book, make a commitment to set aside time to do at least one exercise a day. Are your happiness and your future important enough for you to block out just fifteen minutes daily on your calendar for the next ten days? If so, I guarantee that you'll see positive results.

Self Assessment Questionnaire

Before we begin, I think it's important to have a baseline to know where we're starting from. Use this questionnaire to help evaluate your motivation factors and satisfaction level in your life. Please answer the questions before proceeding with this book.

Circle the option that applies to how you REALLY feel:

Do you get frustrated with your life's challenges?
Never   Rarely   Occasionally   Often   Always

Do you care for others easily, but find it hard to take care of yourself?
Never   Rarely   Occasionally   Often   Always

Do you experience stress in your relationships with others?
Never   Rarely   Occasionally   Often   Always

Do you frequently feel angry or sad?
Never   Rarely   Occasionally   Often   Always

Do you feel unfulfilled in your life, either personally or professionally?
Never   Rarely   Occasionally   Often   Always

Do you feel satisfied with the way you set and reach important goals in your life?
Never   Rarely   Occasionally   Often   Always

Is change difficult for you?
Never   Rarely   Occasionally   Often   Always

Do you recognize and acknowledge your own achievements?
Never   Rarely   Occasionally   Often   Always

Do you experience poor health, fatigue, headaches, aches, or pains?
Never   Rarely   Occasionally   Often   Always

Save these answers. We'll refer to them later.

For an 8 ½ x 11 reprint of all exercises

go to www.AHand bookForLife.com

Do I Have To Struggle?

Chapter goal: Identify your challenges and decide how to handle them.

If things were perfect for you, chances are you wouldn't be reading a book titled *A Handbook for Life*. Life presents us with a series of highs and lows, ups and downs. Where are you on that cycle right now? If you are on the low end you may be asking yourself, "Why do I have to struggle?"

Would your struggles take on a different perspective if you viewed life's circumstances as learning experiences? We grow more as human beings when we face challenges in our life more than we do when things are going well. Accept pain as a catalyst for change. Sometimes you need just a little discomfort to get you to sit down and examine what it is you really want and what you need to change. The challenge in question could be financial. It could be related to problems at work, or a conflict in a personal relationship. Regardless of what our struggles are, after we get through them we usually find that things tend to work out for the best.

I faced a major challenge in my life when I was nineteen. I was a sophomore in college majoring in law enforcement. My lifelong goal was to be an FBI special agent. On November 13, 1975, a day that I will never forget, I was driving to my girlfriend's house on my motorcycle. A car that was heading towards me suddenly turned without signaling and hit me. I wound up in the hospital for three weeks, and was unable to return to school for almost a year. During that time I had six operations and didn't know if I'd ever walk right again. These circumstances forced me to examine my dreams and goals. Everything that I had hoped for in my career path was shattered.

I had a choice. I could wallow in pity or I could face up to the situation I was in and make the most of it. After some investigation and soul searching, I changed my major to computers. Since then I have owned three different computer companies and have enjoyed over thirty years in the computer industry. This industry has been very good to me, and my beautiful wife Marianne of 23 years will tell you very definitely that she would not have married me if I was in the FBI. Looking back now, I know that everything worked out for the best.

Regardless of what your struggle is, when things are tough don't give up. Professor Randy Pausch from *The Last Lecture* says that "Experience is what you get when you get what you didn't want." Accept the challenge when life tests you. Keep your struggles in perspective. Recognize them as opportunities to set new goals and find new ways to achieve them.

DO I HAVE TO STRUGGLE? – EXERCISE:

What challenges are you struggling with right now? Take a few minutes to think of three specific things in your life that aren't working out the way you want them to. On the lines below:

1. List each challenge.

2. Circle the phrase that describes what you want to do about this challenge.

3. Write down how you will follow through with this decision. What specifically will you do to accept or fix the challenge you are experiencing?

1. _____

2. **Accept it** **Fix it**

3. _____

_____

_____

1. _____

2. **Accept it** **Fix it**

3. _____

_____

_____

Richard London

1. _____

2.   **Accept it**   **Fix it**

3. _____

_____

_____

DO I HAVE TO STRUGGLE? – FOLLOW-UP EXERCISE:

You made a good start by identifying three things that are causing stress in your life. Now let me help you deal with that stress.

If you decided to Fix any issue, then start working on the specific actions you wrote down. Begin today. If these actions don't completely resolve your issue, create a plan that will. Include dates by which each action will be completed. Check off each action as you finish it. Revise your plan if necessary, and don't stop until you have reached your goal of having the issue resolved to your satisfaction.

Remember, a perfectly good option is to accept struggle as part of life and not let it bother you. If you decided to accept one or more of the issues above, then don't let them stress you out. Take advantage of the life lessons that are being presented to you. Write down at least three positive aspects of each issue that you are not taking action on.

Issue: _____

1. _____

2. _____

3. _____

Issue: _____

1. _____

2. _____

3. _____

Issue: _____

1. _____

2. _____

3. _____

Who Am I?

Chapter goal: Face who you really are, how others see you, and determine who you would like to be.

Have you ever asked yourself, "Who Am I?" Our society trains us to answer that question by looking outward. Mostly, we define ourselves and others by our roles, occupations, and material possessions.

I used to think of myself only in terms of what I did and how others saw me. When I started my first computer company I was very focused on my image and the image of my company. I felt it was important that other people saw me as a successful businessman. It didn't matter if the company could afford what I spent, I wanted to look successful. One of the first things that I did was lease a company car. Then I bought cars for the service technicians and promptly put the company name on them. I bought mobile phones (the forerunner to cellular phones) for myself and the technicians at a cost of $1000 each. The image I had of myself was centered around what I did for a living, what my hobbies were and what other people thought of me. That thought process resulted in my secretary making more money that I did and me closing the company after only four years.

If I had been asked, "Who are you?" when I was in high school, my answers would have been:

I am male.	I am the oldest of four children.
I am a SCUBA diver.	I am a busboy at a restaurant.
I am the owner of a car.	

If I had been asked, "Who are you?" when I was 32, my answers would have been:

I am married.	I am a father.
I am a pilot.	I am a computer professional.
I am the owner of a house.	

(Actually the bank owned it. I just paid the mortgage and lived there.)

In reality, it is more meaningful to answer the question with answers like:

I am a kind and honest person.

I am a loving parent.

I am a person who is loyal to his friends.

I am a person who tries his best.

I am someone who is improving every day.

When you define yourself by your outward appearance and your material possessions, you set yourself up to live an unfulfilled life. There will always be someone else with more money, nicer clothes, a bigger house and maybe better looks. Why would you let someone else's opinion of you determine how you feel about yourself? Sociologist Judith M. Bardwick says it best: "Real confidence comes from knowing and accepting yourself – your strengths and your limitations – in contrast to depending on affirmation from others."

I'll admit, it's good to have a comfortable home and a nice car, but I realize that happiness comes from within. My wife and I are happy in our lives together because we like who we are. We strive to treat others well and be a good example to our children.

The exercise on the next page is designed to help you think about yourself as a person, not as a father or mother, an employee or a boss, etc.

WHO AM I? – EXERCISE:

How do you think other people see you? Complete the sentence below for each topic listed. Take the time to be honest and thorough. You may notice that these responses might vary if you consider the viewpoints of different people who know you.

When other people describe me in regard to [*topic*] they say I am ...

[Honesty] _____

[Humor] _____

[Loyalty] _____

[Money] _____

[Relationships] _____

[Responsibility] _____

[Sincerity] _____

[Temper] _____

[Trust] _____

Next, we'll take a look at how these answers compare to the way that you would like others to see you. Turn to the next page.

WHO AM I? – EXERCISE Continued:

Now, answer the question, How would you like others to see you? This time, complete the sentence by writing down the ideal personality traits, habits, and attitudes that you *would like* to possess.

When describing the ideal me in regard to [*topic*], I see someone who is ...

[Honesty] _____

[Humor] _____

[Loyalty] _____

[Money] _____

[Relationships] _____

[Responsibility] _____

[Sincerity] _____

[Temper] _____

[Trust] _____

Compare the two lists. Does your vision of the ideal you match up to how you think others see you? If not, what can you do to change? Fill in any of the above areas in which you wish to change, and jot down the actions you will take in each area:

[   ]＿＿＿＿＿＿＿＿＿＿＿＿＿＿＿＿＿＿

[   ]＿＿＿＿＿＿＿＿＿＿＿＿＿＿＿＿＿＿

[   ]＿＿＿＿＿＿＿＿＿＿＿＿＿＿＿＿＿＿

[   ]＿＿＿＿＿＿＿＿＿＿＿＿＿＿＿＿＿＿

[   ]＿＿＿＿＿＿＿＿＿＿＿＿＿＿＿＿＿＿

[   ]＿＿＿＿＿＿＿＿＿＿＿＿＿＿＿＿＿＿

WHO AM I? – FOLLOW-UP EXERCISE:

Do you really want to be the best friend, spouse, or co-worker you can be? Then you need to understand how your friends and spouse *really* perceive you. First, I need to warn you that you need to be ready to hear some things about yourself that you might not like. After all, if each person in your life asked you to tell them the whole truth about how you see him or her, wouldn't you need to list weaknesses as well as strengths?

Ask your friends and spouse to complete the following sentence for each topic:

I would describe [*your name*] in regard to [*topic*] as ...

[Honesty] _____

[Humor] _____

[Loyalty] _____

[Money] _____

[Relationships] _____

[Responsibility] _____

[Sincerity] _____

[Temper] _____

[Trust] _____

WHO AM I? – FOLLOW-UP EXERCISE Continued:

Use the knowledge of how your friends see you to identify how you really come across to others. If the list of your ideal traits and your friends' answers match, congratulations! But if not, then your actions may not be consistent with the "you" that you want to be. Again, fill in any of the areas in which you will work to change, and jot down the actions you will take in each area:

[   ] _____

[   ] _____

[   ] _____

[   ] _____

[   ] _____

[   ] _____

Why Do You Treat Me Like That?

Chapter goal: Improve your relationships with others.

Are you really being as pleasant and respectful to the people around you as you think you are? Are you making yourself loveable? How about at least likeable?

Not long ago I was having problems relating to the people close to me. Marianne and I had a palpable tension between us. My coworkers were cordial, but didn't want to do any more than was necessary to assist me if I needed help. I felt that I wasn't being invited to participate in recreational activities with my friends. I always thought of myself as a loving husband, dependable coworker, and loyal friend. I couldn't figure out why there seemed to be tension in my relationships.

The more I thought about it, the more it occurred to me that I was the problem. I realized that I was not giving the kind of understanding and compassion to others that I expected from them. I was being impatient and demanding. This attitude carried over to work and my home life. The tasks on my agenda had become more important to me than the people around me. Ben Franklin said, "If you would be loved, love and be loveable." After examining the way I was acting, I realized that I was not making myself likeable, let alone loveable.

I made a conscious decision to be more kind and patient with everyone I came in contact with. At home I started out with little gestures. I would give an extra hug to my daughter when I saw her in the morning or passed by her during the day. I would open the car door for Marianne or hold her hand when we were walking out of the movies. I started treating coworkers and friends with more understanding and respect. I actually made a list of positive character traits that I wanted to possess. I wrote the following:

> *I want to be perceived as being:*
> | | |
> |---|---|
> | *Honest* | *Funny* |
> | *Loyal* | *Trustworthy* |
> | *Helpful* | *Dependable* |
> | *Friendly* | *Compassionate* |

Soon I found that people were being more pleasant to me. As soon as I started treating people the way I wanted to be treated I found that my relationships improved and there was less stress in my life. This was the Golden Rule put into action, and it worked better than I imagined in my wildest dreams.

WHY DO YOU TREAT ME LIKE THAT? – EXERCISE:

How would you like to treat other people? Shape your answer to this question into a statement that you can repeat to yourself frequently. This statement, often referred to as an "affirmation," will help you to take the focus off yourself and enable you to appreciate the people around you. Here's mine:

I give thanks to God for the opportunity to serve everyone I come in contact with including my wife, customers, coworkers, family, and friends. I make sure that everyone I come in contact with benefits in some way from our time together.

Why don't you try it? Copy my affirmation above or write one in your own words.

_____

_____

_____

_____

_____

_____

Now repeat this affirmation out loud. I hope you feel a peaceful sensation that you can spread to the people around you.

WHY DO YOU TREAT ME LIKE THAT? – FOLLOW-UP EXERCISE:

Do you really want to get along better with others? The exercise on the previous page is as powerful as it is simple, but it won't do you any good unless you make a decision to make it part of your daily thought process.

Here's how you can make it a habit to remember to treat people better:

1. Take the affirmation you wrote on the previous page and type it into your computer.
2. Print a copy and carry it with you wherever you go.
3. Make a commitment to saying your affirmation *with feeling* at least three times a day for the next week.

I find that the perfect time to read my affirmation is when I am leaving my house or stepping out of my car. It serves as a reminder to treat the people I am about to see the way I want to be treated.

Try this yourself and let me know how it works out. I bet that you'll find that the people around you are magically easier to get along with.

How Can I Control My Anger?

Chapter goal: Learn to stay calm.

Thomas Jefferson said, "If you're angry count to ten before you speak. If you're really angry, count to one hundred." He understood that when we're angry we have a tendency to say and do things we may regret later.

You may not realize that allowing uncontrolled venting of your anger often harms you more than the person or people you may be venting to. Think of the person who gets all worked up while driving in rush hour traffic. He cuts people off, yells, and screams at everyone and no one in particular. By the time he gets where he's going, his blood pressure is through the roof and he is in a foul mood for the rest of the morning.

In the past, I was known to kick and punch holes in walls when I was angry. I got pretty good at repairing sheet rock. It was easier to blame everyone around me for my situation rather than to take responsibility for my actions and reactions.

Recently, the alarm company for my home called me on my cell phone. They told me that the alarm was going off and they had called the police. I thought that my daughter may have left the door ajar when leaving the house. She had done that before. I was on the other side of town, buying sheets of plywood and loading them onto my trailer. I couldn't get home right away. I tried calling my daughter, but she didn't answer her cell phone. I called a neighbor and asked him to meet the police and tell them I was on the way. While I was loading up the trailer and tying down the plywood, my neighbor called three times, wanting to know when I would be there because the police were already there. When I was five minutes from my house, the plywood came loose from the trailer and flew in the air, almost hitting the car behind me. I think you get the picture that this was not a stress-free ride home.

As I was walking through traffic to pick up the plywood and put it back on the trailer, a different neighbor called to tell me the police were at my house. At that point all I could do was laugh out loud. I thought about how comical the whole situation was. I realized that things had spun so far out of control that nothing I could do would fix it. I was being tested and I had to decide how I would deal with the test.

Be mindful of how you react when things are bothering you. Ask yourself, "Is this really worth getting upset about?" Decide if you are in control of your situation or if the situation is in control of you.

Remember that all problems are temporary. Think about the worst problem or embarrassment you ever had. Think about how upset you were. Does that problem still bother you today? Did it still bother you a year after it happened, or even a month later? It's likely that it didn't.

HOW CAN I CONTROL MY ANGER? – EXERCISE:

I'm sure there are things that people around you do from time to time that drive you crazy. Would you like to get a handle on your anger?

Take a few minutes to think of recent incidents when you were frustrated and maybe even lost your temper, or situations that really get you upset every time they come up. Choose three of these to work with. On the lines below:

1. Write down the incident or situation that made you angry.

2. Describe what you could have done to handle the incident or situation without getting upset.

3. List the benefit(s) of handling the incident in a calmer manner.

1. Incident: _____

2. I could have... _____

3. Benefit(s): _____

_____

1. Incident: _____

2. I could have... _____

3. Benefit(s): _____

_____

1. Incident:

2. I could have…

3. Benefit(s):

HOW CAN I CONTROL MY ANGER? – FOLLOW-UP EXERCISE:

Whenever something happens to get you upset, try counting to ten before reacting. (Yes, you've heard this before, and I'm telling you again because it really does work.) While you're counting start asking yourself questions like, "Will I still be upset about this tomorrow?" "What part did I play in this?" "What is there to be gained by my yelling?" And, "How will my reaction reflect my love for the person, or people, around me?"

Will you agree that it takes a stronger person to control their temper than to lose it? Take pride in your ability to show restraint.

How Can I Be Success-Minded?

Chapter goal: Create a positive mental attitude and learn to overcome challenges.

To create the right environment to succeed, you need to do everything possible to cut negativity out of your life. The bigger your goal, the more careful you must be about maintaining a positive focus at all times. Be careful about who you share your goals with. The most well meaning friends and relatives can shoot down your ideas and burst your bubble before you know it. This can apply to the goal of starting a new business, starting an exercise program, or even quitting smoking.

Negativity can be contagious, but so is success. When I decided to begin investing in real estate, I only listened to the advice of people who were already successful real estate investors. I joined a real estate investors group to be around other like-minded people. I realized that the gloom and doom that permeated the news would do nothing to help me succeed in my new venture. As a result, I stopped watching the news on TV and stopped focusing on the negative stories in the newspaper. You may have heard of other people who have cut the media out of their lives and not understood why they did it, but speaking for myself, I found it a crucial part of remaining positive and not letting others tear down my dream.

Maintaining a positive attitude alone will not keep you from encountering challenges. You have to be willing to do what it takes to overcome obstacles. When I was in my twenties, I earned a second degree black belt in Tae Kwon Do. I experienced a number of setbacks and injuries along the way, but nothing like what I experienced at age 46 when I took on a similar goal. I had been training in Kempo, a physically demanding martial art, for about five years. My instructor was just getting ready to announce the date for my black belt test. I was slower, less agile, and had more balance problems than when I was younger, but I worked hard to get my 46-year-old body in shape. Then my old motorcycle injury started bothering me and I needed to undergo three operations on my leg.

How badly did I want this black belt? I was committed to it and never considered backing away from my goal. It took me six months to regain my strength for the black belt test, but I finally earned my black belt in Kempo. It wasn't until a few years later, when I was diagnosed with Parkinson's disease, that I found out why I had been having problems with my balance.

Anything worth having is worth working for. Professor Randy Pausch says that "Brick walls are there to show us how badly we want something." When things get tough, expect obstacles, but don't let them get in your way. Henry Ford said, "Obstacles are those frightful things you see when you take your eyes off your goal."

When you write down your goals ask yourself, "What would I do if I was guaranteed that I could not fail?" Let yourself get emotional about what your life will be like when you achieve your goals.

HOW CAN I BE SUCCESS-MINDED? – EXERCISE:

What is the most important goal in your life right now? Write it down as a positive statement as if it has already happened.

_____

_____

Now make a list of every resource you can think of that provides the support and knowledge necessary to be successful in reaching that goal. Think of support groups, books, mentor programs, professional coaches, etc.

_____

_____

_____

_____

_____

_____

_____

_____

_____

Now, pick at least one resource off this list. Write it down below along with a date that you will start using that resource to help achieve your goal.

_____

_____

HOW CAN I BE SUCCESS-MINDED? – FOLLOW-UP EXERCISE:

Success is a thought process that can only exist in a positive mind. Are you serious about staying positive and focused on your goals? If so, can you make a commitment to yourself to not watch the news for a week? OK, you can watch the weather, but as soon as a negative news story comes on turn off the TV or change the channel. And, I strongly recommend that you do not watch TV before going to bed. If you have to do something to clear your mind, then read a positive, inspiring book for fifteen minutes.

If reading the newspaper is part of your regular routine, then skim the paper for topics that interest you, but don't read the negative articles.

I predict that by the end of the week, two things will happen. First, you will realize how addicted you have been to the mental stimulation of negative events. Second, you will be more conscious of your thought processes and will begin protecting your mind from negative influences.

What Do I Want Out Of Life?

Chapter goal: Evaluate what will make you happy and formulate a plan to bring more fulfillment into your life.

Have you thought recently about what would make your life more fulfilling? Are you satisfied with your job, your personal relationships, your physical body? I find that I'm constantly evaluating the different areas of my life. If I'm dissatisfied with something I frequently ask, "What can I change to improve this situation?"

I value my happiness, and most importantly, I believe that I deserve to be happy. You deserve to be happy, too, and you have the power to bring that happiness to yourself. Start today by asking, "What would make my life more rewarding?" Take a close look at all aspects of your life: work, education, recreation, finances, and personal relationships. Do you like where you live? Is your job giving you the satisfaction you want? Are you saving enough money? Is your social life satisfying?

I've found that people are too quick to settle for average. Set goals for the changes you want to make, then break these goals into short, medium, and long range. Short range may be next week, next month, or within the next six months, depending on the goal and how it fits into your life. Medium range may be six months to a year, and long range may be three to five years.

Next set a plan for meeting these goals. Many people have goals, but never write down a plan to reach them. Writing down your goals AND a plan to reach them provides a framework to operate in. You wouldn't think of building a house without a blueprint, so why would you plan your life without one?

I create a plan for virtually everything I do. I evaluate my plan on a regular basis and am willing to make adjustments if I don't see the results I anticipated. Expect challenges along the way and keep focused on your goals. It's amazing what you accomplish when you have a vision and make the effort to put it into action.

WHAT DO I WANT OUT OF LIFE? – EXERCISE:

People's actions are generally based on either seeking pleasure or avoiding pain. The goals we set for ourselves work the same way. Answer the following questions in as many different ways as you can.

I am happiest when:

_____

_____

_____

_____

_____

I am frustrated when:

_____

_____

_____

_____

_____

When you think about the goals you have in your life, do you see a correlation to what you wrote above? If you can't think of any goals that you currently have, then take a closer look at what you wrote down here. Use these answers to help you determine what goals you may start working towards to bring you happiness and a more fulfilled life. Why don't you write them down while you're thinking about them?

WHAT DO I WANT OUT OF LIFE? – FOLLOW-UP EXERCISE:

NOTE: This is the most important exercise in this book for setting goals. If you really want to change things in your life then be ready to set aside 20 – 30 minutes to identify your goal and begin implementing your game plan for achieving it.

This exercise is designed to guide you through setting goals and reaching them easily. You can use this technique repeatedly in different areas of your life for short, medium, and long range goals. It is my hope that you become comfortable with the process and repeat it regularly.

Follow these steps to succeed in any venture:
1. **Identify your goal.**
2. **If needed, find people who are already successful in this area and learn from them.**
3. **Create a game plan for your success.**
4. **Remove negative influences from your life.**
5. **Stay focused and work your plan.**
6. **Expect obstacles and persevere.**
7. **Evaluate your progress on a regular basis.**
8. **Continue to adapt and work your plan until you succeed.**

1. Identify your goal. For the purposes of this exercise, answer the questions below about your job, your health, and your relationships. You will then pick one area to concentrate on.

At my job I'm frustrated when:

Concerning my health, I'm frustrated when:

_____

_____

Concerning my relationships, I'm frustrated when:

_____

_____

Write down what you would like to change in each area within the next 30 days.

What I really want to change about my job is:

_____

_____

What I really want to change about my health is:

_____

_____

What I really want to change about my relationships is:

_____

_____

Now pick one of the three statements about what you want to change above and write what you will change in the next 30 days.

_____

_____

_____

2. If needed, find people who are already successful in this area and learn from them. Ask yourself if you need any additional training to accomplish your goal. Can you find a mentor to guide you? Should you enroll in a course, join a support group, or read books on the subject? Write down what, if any, additional training you may require:

_____

_____

_____

3. Create a game plan for your success. How will you accomplish your goal? What will you do differently over the next 30 days to achieve your desired result? Make a list and be as specific as you can be.

_____

_____

_____

_____

_____

_____

The steps above helped you to identify your goal and create a plan to achieve it. Now, apply the steps below on a daily basis to follow through with your plan.

4. Remove negative influences from your life. You already understand the importance of maintaining a positive frame of mind. Avoid negative influences in your life, including people who do not support you.

5. Stay focused and work your plan. Write down your goals and the rewards that will come to you when you achieve them.

_____

_____

_____

_____

Reread your goals several times each day to keep yourself focused on your plan. Make time every day to do something to work towards your goal.

6. Expect obstacles and persevere. Don't be surprised when you encounter obstacles. Remind yourself of the rewards that are waiting for you when you achieve your goals:

_____

_____

7. Evaluate your progress on a regular basis. You may find that you are not achieving your goals as quickly as you expected. Be willing to evaluate your plan and make adjustments as necessary.

8. Continue to adapt and work your plan until you succeed.
Perseverance is the key. Reread your goals on a daily basis. Stay focused, expect obstacles, and revise your plan as needed.

Now you have a framework to begin changing your life. The decision to follow through is up to you.

Is Now Really The Right Time To Begin?

Chapter goal: Make the decision to take action now.

What excuses have you been using to justify why you haven't started working towards your goals? Do you find it difficult to get out of your comfort zone even when you know that you want to improve something in your life? When I started investing in real estate, virtually all of my friends agreed it was a good idea. Most of them admitted they needed more money and security for retirement. Many of them said they had thought about investing in real estate themselves.

I started reading books and attending seminars. After just a few months I bought my first foreclosure property. As I began taking action, people around me came up with more and more reasons why they couldn't do what I was doing. The two major justifications I kept hearing were that they didn't have enough time or they didn't have enough money. Well, I had less time and money than most of them.

After a year or so, my friends said to me, "You were able to buy those houses because you got into the housing market at the right time. Things are different now." Well, I learned that timing doesn't matter. The only day that matters is the day you decide to take action.

Coach Vincent Williams, author of *How Do I Reach My True Destiny,* says, "Change is a process, but the decision to change happens in an instant." When are you going to decide to make changes in your life? Procrastination is your enemy. No, the exercise program can't wait until the weekend. Your diet shouldn't start after the holidays are over, and there's no benefit to begin looking for a better job after the summer is over. The problem with waiting until this weekend, January first, or the end of summer vacation is that dates come and go, but the decision to make life changes just goes.

Ask yourself why you want to exercise, lose weight, get a better job, or whatever. How long have you been unhappy with that area of your life? Will things improve if you continue to delay making a change? Practice action-oriented thinking. I have a philosophy, "98% of the time the easy decision to not do anything is the wrong decision." Think about this, if you don't make a change now, then what will be different six months, one year, or five years from now? I think you know the answer.

IS NOW REALLY THE RIGHT TIME TO BEGIN? – EXERCISE:

Do you really want to make positive changes in your life? If so, what's stopping you from beginning to make those changes today? In the exercise from the chapter *How Can I Be Success-Minded?* you wrote down your most important goal. What, you still haven't done the exercise? How do you expect to reach your goals if you don't write them down? This time try writing your most important goal as if it already happened, and assign a completion date to it. For example: *I am so proud and happy that I lost 20 pounds by March 15th*.

Rewrite your goal now as if it already happened and assign a completion date to it.

Now write down all of the advantages and positive things that you will have and experience when you achieve your goal. Really think this through. The more exciting the rewards, the quicker you will reach your goal. Finish the following sentence.

Because I achieved my goal I...

Now write down what actions you are taking today to achieve this goal.

To reach my goal, today I will...

_____

_____

_____

_____

IS NOW REALLY THE RIGHT TIME TO BEGIN? – FOLLOW-UP EXERCISE:

You did a great job writing down your goal, target date, and benefits of achieving your goal. Read over your goal and the benefits on a regular basis. Keep yourself motivated and excited about achieving your dream, and keep planning and taking actions toward your goal.

Do you have trouble getting even your small, daily tasks accomplished? Try this. Either first thing in the morning or just before you go to bed make a list of everything you need to get done in the next 24 hours. Prioritize the list in order of importance.

Refer to the list constantly throughout the day. Your goal should be to resolve every item on the list that day. Here's a tip: When possible, do the hardest or least fun items first. That way they will be off the list and you will have a real sense of relief and accomplishment that will encourage you to do more.

Why Do I Have To Delay My Rewards?

Chapter goal: Understand the need to delay gratification.

Wouldn't it be nice if your employer paid you in advance every Monday morning, before the work week started? Maybe colleges should give out degrees on the first day of classes without waiting for students to study for four years. These scenarios sound rather bizarre, don't they? We inherently understand that we have to invest time, money, and mental effort to reap rewards in life. So why is it that so many people are unwilling to delay their gratification to achieve personal goals?

I can't think of any endeavor in life that doesn't require work before success is achieved. After my motorcycle accident, I changed my major in college to computer science, but every time I faced a job change I considered returning to law enforcement. When I was 34, I sat down with Marianne and poured my heart out. I explained that my lifelong goal was to go into the FBI and that if I didn't at least try to get in, I would never be happy. She wasn't pleased, but she loved me enough not to stand in my way.

Getting accepted into the FBI is a year-long process. I submitted a twenty page application, then took a written test and passed it. I had a panel interview with three special agents and passed the interview. That's when Marianne sat me down and poured *her* heart out. She was not happy with my decision. She did not want to be told by the federal government when we would have to move and where we would live for the rest of our lives. I understood how she felt, but I still ached to be involved in law enforcement. After giving it a lot of thought, I proposed a compromise.

In the state of North Carolina, police departments can hire part-time officers, and you can enroll in the police academy before you are hired by a department. I suggested that I withdraw my application to the FBI, but work part-time for a local police department. I knew that Marianne was not thrilled with that idea either, but in her mind it was the lesser of two evils, so she agreed.

I was able to get sponsored into the police academy by the local sheriff's department. That's when the sacrifice began. At the time, I had a full time job, a house, a two-year-old son, and a baby was on the way. North Carolina Basic Law Enforcement Training was a four-month program. I was in class or on the shooting range from 6:00pm to 10:00pm Monday through Friday and 8:00am to 4:00pm on Saturdays from September through December 1990.

It was a total disruption of my life, and my wife's as well. During those four months I gave up all of my free time on evenings and weekends. I turned down invitations to do things with friends. I was totally focused on excelling at the academy. Was it worth it? I graduated second in my class on what was one of the proudest and happiest days of my life. How did Marianne feel about my basically not being available for four months? Did she understand the need to give up something in the short term to achieve a long term goal? Well, my wonderful wife not only sacrificed her spare time and social life, she celebrated my graduation by throwing a surprise party for me. No wonder we're still happily married after 23 years.

Most of your dreams and goals won't require that you stop all recreational activities and dedicate six days a week to their fulfillment, but would you be willing to do so if that's what was needed? If you are willing to tolerate short-term sacrifices, you will enjoy long-term rewards.

WHY DO I HAVE TO DELAY MY REWARDS? – EXERCISE:

How do you spend your time and what activities would you be willing to give up temporarily in order to reach your dreams and goals? Think about your average week. Write down all the activities that you do, even sleeping. Include your time working, eating, bathing, running errands, watching TV, playing sports, attending recreational events, spending time with your family, doing household chores, etc. Consider your work days and your weekends. Then write down on each line the number of hours a week on average that you spend in each activity.

Activity   **Hours/Week**

_____   _____

_____   _____

_____   _____

_____   _____

_____   _____

_____   _____

_____   _____

_____   _____

Total hours   _____

Just for curiosity's sake, how close did you get to the 168 hours in an actual week?

To get the most out of this exercise, review the list and determine what activities take time away from achieving your goals. What are you willing to cut back on temporarily to realize your dreams? Circle these activities and replace the number of hours you're currently spending on this activity with the number of hours you will spend (maybe it's 0 now). You may see that delaying your gratification is not as big a sacrifice as you thought it would be. How many hours have you freed up to achieve your goal? _____

WHY DO I HAVE TO DELAY MY REWARDS? – FOLLOW UP EXERCISE:

In the first exercise of this chapter, you estimated where your time was spent. But how do you really spend your time? If you're serious about understanding how much time you're devoting to activities that you can cut back on, then you need to keep a time log for a week. Start by writing down the activities you identified in the previous exercise. Leave room next to each activity to list the time you spend doing it. Every day for a week, write down the time you start each activity, the time you finish it, and the total time spent on the activity. If an activity you engage in is not on the list, add it. Make extra copies of this page if necessary.

Day	Activity	Start	End	Total

At the end of the week, add up the total amount of time spent on each activity. Now, review your list and decide what activities you can temporarily cut back on, or even eliminate, to make your dreams a reality.

How much time each week will you invest in achieving your goals?

_____

On what days and at what time? _____

Who/What Is God?

Chapter goal: Build a spiritual base to better deal with people and to persevere when times get tough.

God is one of the most controversial subjects in the world, but I would be doing you a great disservice if I let this fact intimidate me and omitted this chapter. I don't want to preach to you or promote any specific religion. Needless to say, each individual's faith is very personal and not only varies from religion to religion, but also from person to person within the same church, synagogue, temple, or mosque. My focus here is on how our belief in God, a creator, or the universal life force can affect our daily lives. I just want to convey a simple point about the value of developing a spiritual foundation as a component of your thought process. I've found it helpful to use that foundation as a guide to building relationships with others and as a support to lean on when times get tough.

Everything we do affects someone else. We are all faced with situations each day where we must coexist with another person. All major religions have rules for getting along with other people. Belief in God gives us a blueprint for right and wrong and allows us to feel we are part of a bigger whole. Society cannot live without rules. The result would be anarchy and chaos. Use your belief in some power or principle larger than yourself to remind yourself that there is an overriding good that you can reference. This will guide your words and actions regarding the people you come in contact with each day. That overriding good can make you a better neighbor, coworker, parent, child, and friend.

Also, when we try to solve all of our problems ourselves the stress can be overwhelming. Quite often I find that my frustration comes from trying to change a situation that is out of my control. Being able to release the challenges of life to a higher power can be a very liberating experience. By realizing that we can call on the assistance of a higher power for help, we are able to let go of pressures that, many times, are self-imposed. As a result, we find it easier to persevere and overcome the situations that confront and challenge us.

WHO/WHAT IS GOD? – EXERCISE:

Your beliefs are your own. It is not my place to tell you how you should relate to God, or even if you should believe that a God exists. But, I have found that believing in and communicating with a higher power has given me the serenity and confidence I have needed to live a successful life.

Here are some questions relating to your spiritual life for you to consider. Ask yourself:

Do I have dreams and goals in my life that   Yes   No
are unfulfilled?

Could I use some outside help in my life?   Yes   No

Do I have conflicts with people that at times
are difficult to resolve?   Yes   No

Would it hurt if I asked a higher power for
guidance?   Yes   No

Could it help?   Yes   No

Who are three people I feel comfortable talking with about God?

_____

_____

_____

How do you think that a higher power can help and support you in your life? Are you willing to talk with someone else about how you envision a higher power in your life? Try using the questions above to start a conversation with someone you are comfortable talking with.

WHO/WHAT IS GOD? – FOLLOW-UP EXERCISE:

Use these activities if you want to strengthen your relationship with God as you understand him. Again, I'm not here to preach. If you're not comfortable with this topic, go to the next chapter.

1. If you are interested, join a discussion group or evening course at your place of worship.
2. Have an honest discussion about God with your spouse or a close friend. Don't let the fear of causing an argument stand in your way. Instead concentrate on understanding each other's point of view and broadening your views.
3. Start and end each day by having a personal discussion with God as you understand him. Begin the talk by giving thanks for all of the good things in your life. That will open up your mind and spirit. Then talk to him about what is on your mind.

Why Pay Attention To My Physical Health?

*Chapter goal: Cultivate a healthy body
to cultivate a healthy mind.*

I bet that, at least a few times in the past 30 days, you told yourself that you were going to exercise regularly, eat less, quit smoking, or do something similarly noble. So what if you didn't exactly follow through? What's the harm? Well, your physical health is directly tied to your emotional health.

Look at yourself as a complete person: mind, body, heart, and soul. Keeping one part sharp automatically improves the other parts. Settling for feeling adequate instead of great is no way to go through life. If you don't like the way you feel about yourself, then you can't like the way you feel about others.

I am probably a lot like you. Over my lifetime, I have varied greatly in my dedication to my physical health. I have gone from being a physical fanatic to working out maybe twice a week, from exercising daily to going months without any physical activity at all. The one thing that I can tell you is that no matter how lazy or down I felt before I exercised, I always felt better after I worked out.

Daily physical exercise is important to release stress. When your body is moving, you have the opportunity to clear your mind. I find that when I am running on the treadmill and my body is alert, my mind is as well. Quite frequently a solution to a problem or a new approach to a situation comes to me while I'm exercising. I use this time to help crystallize my goals and focus on a positive attitude. I don't run on the treadmill with the TV on. I especially don't watch the news while I exercise.

Before I start exercising, I frequently recite my daily affirmation. This helps get me in a positive frame of mind and opens my subconscious to creative thoughts. I usually listen to music while I work out, but it's music with a twist. I put my MP3 player on random search and intersperse music with my favorite motivational speakers. That way, I hear a song or two and then a positive motivational message. Exercising like that frequently produces some of the best solutions to my problems.

Is it easy to exercise three times a week? Is it easy to get an adequate amount of sleep each night? Is it easy to lose 20 pounds? Is it easy to quit smoking? Of course not, but you know you'll feel better after you do. Take little steps to get started. Instead of jogging for thirty minutes, put on your running shoes and go for a fifteen-minute walk.

Take care of yourself. Be good to your body. Get enough rest *today*. Start that diet *today*, exercise *today*, find a friend to help you quit smoking *today*. Your health affects your happiness. Don't put it off. It's not that big a chore if you take it one day at a time, and the benefits far outweigh the effort.

WHY PAY ATTENTION TO MY PHYSICAL HEALTH? – EXERCISE:

If you're like me, you've probably made and broken dozens of promises to yourself over the years when it comes to taking care of your health. So why is this time any different? Well, after completing the work in the previous chapters, I think you are better prepared to set goals and follow through with them. Don't you?

Take a few minutes and write down three goals you have for better physical health. The goal could be about exercising, losing weight, eating better, quitting smoking, or whatever matters to you.

1. _____

2. _____

3. _____

Now, pick one small step you can take *today* to put each of these goals in motion in your life.

1. _____

2. _____

3. _____

WHY PAY ATTENTION TO MY PHYSICAL HEALTH?
– FOLLOW-UP EXERCISE:

Pick the most important of the three goals from the previous page. Can you make a promise to yourself to set up a program to follow through on that goal? You know how; just follow the steps from the Follow-up Exercise in the chapter *What Do I Want Out of Life?* Once you are on the way to reaching this goal, then set a plan to achieve the next one.

Start with small time commitments if you have to. By the end of three weeks, you will have established a new, healthy habit.

Self Assessment Questionnaire Follow-up

This is the same questionnaire you filled out before you read this book and worked through the exercises. Please answer the questions without referring to your previous answers.

Circle the option that applies to how you REALLY feel:

Do you get frustrated with your life's challenges?
Never   Rarely   Occasionally   Often   Always

Do you care for others easily, but find it hard to take care of yourself?
Never   Rarely   Occasionally   Often   Always

Do you experience stress in your relationships with others?
Never   Rarely   Occasionally   Often   Always

Do you frequently feel angry or sad?
Never   Rarely   Occasionally   Often   Always

Do you feel unfulfilled in your life, either personally or professionally?
Never   Rarely   Occasionally   Often   Always

Do you feel satisfied with the way you set and reach important goals in your life?
Never   Rarely   Occasionally   Often   Always

Is change difficult for you?
Never   Rarely   Occasionally   Often   Always

Do you recognize and acknowledge your own achievements?
Never   Rarely   Occasionally   Often   Always

Do you experience poor health, fatigue, headaches, aches, or pains?

Never   Rarely   Occasionally   Often   Always

Now compare the answers above with your previous responses. Do you see any differences? Are there areas of your life that you feel you would like to continue improving on? I hope that I have helped you get started on your journey to a happier and more successful life. Be sure to let me know how you do.

Tell Me, Why Did I Read This Book?

We all have areas of our lives that aren't quite the way we'd like them to be. We have up times and down times, mountains and valleys. During the up times, we feel good about ourselves, our families and our relationships. When things are going smoothly, we're able to relax and coast through the day.

The problem is that on the down days, the days that frustrate us, we have a tendency to feel helpless. When there are money problems we complain, "I don't understand what's wrong, I'm working as hard as I can." When we gain a couple extra pounds we look in the mirror and say, "I just can't seem to keep the weight off." When our children misbehave we say, "What am I going to do? They never listen to me." During these times we often miss the opportunity to pause, reflect, and reconsider our professional and personal paths.

You read *A Handbook for Life* because empowering yourself begins with knowing who you are and what you want. You learned to like yourself and get control of your life. You got control by taking responsibility for your thoughts and attitudes. You took time to count your blessings and know your strengths.

A Handbook for Life gave you the tools to build the best possible life for yourself. Don't delay one minute.

As you continue to recognize areas of your life that you want to improve, immediately write down the changes you would like to make. Then set a time to start implementing those changes.

Look at how far you've already come: You've become more tolerant of others. You recognize that you make mistakes every day of your life, and now that you realize that no one is perfect, life is much less stressful for you and those around you. Now that you better understand yourself and strive to be a better person every day, you truly hold the key to happiness in life.

THE REAL FOLLOW-UP EXERCISE:

Now that you've read this book, take one more step for your personal development. Are you ready? Good. Go back and review the results of the exercises. What? You didn't do all of the exercises? Well, that's OK, but now it's "catch up" time. Review the exercises from each chapter or do them for the first time. Read them over with the mindset that you are ready to take action and be a happier, more fulfilled you.

To get the most value from this book, commit to redoing at least one exercise each week. You'll find that, as you refresh the concepts and activities in your mind on a regular basis, you will continue to transform.

I hope that you find yourself increasingly more productive, more relaxed, less stressed and closer to the people around you. Remember, the time to take action is NOW.

Author's Note

This book is the first in a series. I hope you found it useful. For more information about the concepts in this book and the *A Handbook for Life*^{SM} seminars, go to www.AHandbookForLife. com.

Please look for these additional titles in the future:

A Handbook for Friends

A Handbook for Personal Relationships

A Handbook for Business Relationships

A Handbook for Parents

A Handbook for Employees

Best wishes in all you do.

Sincerely,

Rich

Rich London may be contacted for speaking engagements and seminars by emailing rlondon@AHandbookForLife.com